**STORY BY
DAN JOLLEY**

**PENCILS AND INKS BY
RON RANDALL**

THIS MAP SHOWS CHINA AS IT LOOKED
AT THE END OF THE HAN DYNASTY
(206 B.C. TO A.D. 220).

GUAN YU

BLOOD BROTHERS TO THE END

N

Yellow River

CHINA

LUOYANG

XIAPI

YUZHOU

HANZHONG

JINGZHOU

A CHINESE LEGEND

XIANGYANG

YIZHOU

JIANGLING

GRAPHIC UNIVERSE™ MINNEAPOLIS • NEW YORK

GUAN YU WAS AN ANCIENT CHINESE WARRIOR. HE IS ALSO AN IMPORTANT FIGURE IN *THE ROMANCE OF THE THREE KINGDOMS*, A FOURTEENTH-CENTURY NOVEL ATTRIBUTED TO CHINESE WRITER LUO GUANZHONG. LUO'S NOVEL DESCRIBES THE ACTIVITIES OF WARRIORS IN THE YEARS FOLLOWING THE HAN DYNASTY (206 B.C. TO A.D. 220).

THIS ADAPTATION OF GUAN YU'S STORY IS BASED PRIMARILY ON *THREE KINGDOMS: A HISTORICAL NOVEL*, TRANSLATED BY MOSS ROBERTS. IT WAS WRITTEN IN CONSULTATION WITH WANG PING, PHD, ASSOCIATE PROFESSOR OF ENGLISH AT MACALESTER COLLEGE, AND WEN-HUA DU, MA, OF THE DEPARTMENT OF FOREIGN LANGUAGES AND LINGUISTICS AT THE UNIVERSITY OF WISCONSIN–MILWAUKEE. THE ARTWORK FOR THE BOOK IS BASED ON NUMEROUS HISTORICAL RESOURCES AND WAS REVIEWED FOR ACCURACY BY WANG PING.

STORY BY DAN JOLLEY

PENCILS AND INKS BY RON RANDALL

COLORING BY HI-FI COLOUR DESIGN

LETTERING BY MARSHALL DILLON
AND TERRI DELGADO

CONSULTANTS: WANG PING, PHD,
ASSOCIATE PROFESSOR OF ENGLISH,
MACALESTER COLLEGE,
AND WEN-HUA DU, MA,
DEPARTMENT OF FOREIGN LANGUAGES AND
LINGUISTICS, UNIVERSITY OF WISCONSIN–MILWAUKEE

Graphic Universe™
A division of Lerner Publishing Group, Inc.
241 First Avenue North
Minneapolis, MN 55401 U.S.A.

Website address: www.lernerbooks.com

Library of Congress Cataloging-in-Publication Data

Jolley, Dan.
    Guan Yu : blood brothers to the end : a Chinese legend / story by Dan Jolley ; pencils and inks by Ron Randall.
        p.   cm. — (Graphic myths and legends)
    Includes index.
        ISBN-13: 978-0-8225-7527-6 (lib. bdg. : alk. paper)
        1. Luo, Guanzhong, ca. 1330-ca. 1400. San guo zhi yan yi. 2. Guan, Yu, 160-220—Fiction. 3. China—History—Three kingdoms, 220-265—Fiction. I. Randall, Ron. II. Title.
    PL2690.S33J65 2008
    741.5'973—dc22   2007019742

Manufactured in the United States of America
1 2 3 4 5 6 - JR - 13 12 11 10 09 08

TABLE OF CONTENTS

THE LEGEND BEGINS

WHAT'S THIS STATUE, GRANDPA?

THAT'S *GUAN YU.*

A LOT OF PEOPLE CALL HIM A GOD OF *WAR.* BUT WHAT GUAN YU TRULY STANDS FOR IS HONOR AND RIGHTEOUSNESS AND *BROTHERHOOD.*

THERE ARE MANY STORIES ABOUT GUAN YU ... FANTASTICAL STORIES OF HIM FIGHTING *DEMONS.*

BUT MY FAVORITE ONES ARE A LITTLE MORE DOWN TO EARTH.

WAS GUAN YU *REAL*? LIKE, A REAL GUY?

OH, YES. YES, HE WAS VERY REAL. GUAN YU AND HIS TWO *BLOOD BROTHERS,* LIU BEI AND ZHANG FEI.

IT ALL STARTED JUST ABOUT TWO THOUSAND YEARS AGO, IN CHINA ...

When Guan Yu was a young man—barely twenty-three years old—he had some trouble in his hometown ...

... so he set out to seek his fortune someplace else.

Eventually he arrived in a small town in northern China and decided to stop in a tavern for something to drink.

Inside the tavern, Guan Yu met two men who would change his life forever: *LIU BEI* and *ZHANG FEI*.

They had just begun *RECRUITING* men to help them fight a group of *REBELS* called the *YELLOW SCARVES*.

Liu Bei invited Guan Yu to join them, and very soon, Guan Yu agreed to fight by their side to put down the rebellion.

BEFORE LONG, THEY FACED A THREAT OF A DIFFERENT NATURE. IN THE CAPITAL CITY, *LUOYANG*, THE EMPEROR XIAN HAD GROWN WEAK ...

... AND AN EVIL MAN CALLED *DONG ZHUO* HAD TAKEN CONTROL OF HIM.

WARLORDS FROM ACROSS THE COUNTRY CAME TOGETHER TO OPPOSE DONG ZHUO ...

... BUT THE FIRST THING THEY HAD TO DO WAS MAKE THEIR WAY THROUGH THE *SI RIVER PASS*, A NARROW CORRIDOR THROUGH THE MOUNTAINS.

AND DONG ZHUO HAD POSTED A *GUARDIAN* THERE IN THE PASS.

HIS NAME WAS *HUA XIONG* ... AND HE HAD ALREADY *KILLED* FOUR OF THE WARLORDS: BAO ZHONG, ZU MAO, YU SHE, AND PAN FENG.

HUA XIONG SEEMED *UNSTOPPABLE*, AND THE WARLORDS WERE RELUCTANT TO GO UP AND FACE HIM.

11

BLOOD BROTHERS UNITED

GUAN YU AND ZHANG FEI FOUGHT FOR LIU BEI IN MANY BATTLES, PROVING THEMSELVES TO BE FEARSOME WARRIORS.

SOON LIU BEI BECAME GOVERNOR OF PINGYUAN COUNTY. QUICKLY HE PROMOTED GUAN YU AND ZHANG FEI TO COMMANDERS.

NO MATTER HOW DANGEROUS THINGS BECAME, GUAN YU AND ZHANG FEI STUCK WITH LIU BEI.

THEY HAD SWORN TO FOLLOW HIM UNQUESTIONINGLY AND TO PROTECT HIM FROM EVERY THREAT.

NOT LONG AFTERWARD, LIU BEI ASSASSINATED THE GOVERNOR OF THE XUZHOU REGION AND RODE INTO THE CAPITAL CITY, *XIAPI*, WITH HIS BROTHERS.

LOOK AT THE PEOPLE, LIU BEI. THEY ARE *TERRIFIED* OF YOU.

THAT THEY MAY BE.

WHICH IS WHY I AM PUTTING *YOU* IN CONTROL OF XIAPI.

EXCUSE ME?

LIU BEI WAS QUITE SERIOUS. HE LEFT GUAN YU IN CHARGE OF THE CITY—AND ASKED HIM TO WATCH OVER HIS TWO *WIVES* AS WELL.

THEN LIU BEI DEPARTED, FOR HE HAD BUSINESS TO TAKE CARE OF IN THE NEARBY CITY OF *XIAOPEI*.

BUT WHAT NONE OF THE BROTHERS HAD COUNTED ON WAS THE EFFECT THIS TAKEOVER WOULD HAVE ON *CAO CAO*, WHO WAS CLOSE TO THE CITY'S FORMER GOVERNOR.

HOW *DARE* THEY?

MOBILIZE THE TROOPS *IMMEDIATELY!*

13

SOON CAO CAO'S ARMY WAS ON THE MARCH, HEADED EAST INTO XUZHOU ...

... AND THEIR FIRST OBJECTIVE WAS THE CAPITAL: XIAPI.

A NEW ALLEGIANCE

GUAN YU SERVED CAO CAO WELL, BUT SOON A SERIOUS PROBLEM AROSE.

LIU BEI AND ZHANG FEI HAD FLED NORTH AND JOINED WITH THE FEARSOME WARLORD *YUAN SHAO*.

AND IT WASN'T LONG BEFORE YUAN SHAO SENT HIS OWN ARMY TO ATTACK CAO CAO.

GUAN YU JUDGED YAN LIANG'S TROOPS WELL. SO FEROCIOUS WAS HIS CHARGE ...

... THAT THE ENEMY SOLDIERS PARTED BEFORE HIM LIKE WHEAT IN A STRONG WIND.

THE STORY WAS SIMILAR WHEN THEY REACHED XINGYANG ... BUT ON A GRANDER SCALE.

RIGHT THIS WAY, GUAN YU.

TRAVELING WITH SUCH PRECIOUS WOMEN, SURELY YOU WANT TO GIVE THEM A WARM, SAFE PLACE TO REST FOR THE NIGHT.

THANK YOU, GOVERNOR WANG. YOU SPEAK WISELY. I ACCEPT YOUR OFFER.

THIS JOURNEY HAS BEEN DIFFICULT AND FILLED WITH TREACHERY.

LIKE BIAN XI, GOVERNOR WANG ZHI PLANNED TO WAIT UNTIL GUAN YU WAS ASLEEP TO ATTACK HIM.

HE FELT A *THOUSAND* MEN WOULD SURELY BE ABLE TO SET THE BUILDING ON FIRE AND BURN GUAN YU TO DEATH IN HIS SLEEP.

BUT HU BAN, AIDE TO GOVERNOR WANG, HAD GROWN CURIOUS. GUAN YU WAS FAMOUS, AND HU BAN WANTED A BETTER LOOK AT THE MAN.

BLOOD BROTHERS
ONCE MORE

*T*HE MEETING, WHEN IT FINALLY TOOK PLACE, WAS A *JOYOUS* OCCASION. HAPPINESS OVERCAME GUAN YU WHEN HE AND HIS BLOOD BROTHERS REUNITED.

BUT THEY WERE NOT TO KNOW PEACE. EVEN AS GUAN YU FOUND LIU BEI AND ZHANG FEI ...

... CAO CAO HAD MOBILIZED HIS ARMY AND BEGUN TO MARCH AGAINST YUAN SHAO.

YUAN SHAO WAS EAGER TO FACE CAO CAO'S FORCES AND SENT HIS OWN ARMY INTO BATTLE.

IN THE WAKE OF THIS MASSIVE VICTORY, LIU BEI SENT GUAN YU TO THE CITY OF *XIANGYANG.*

LIU BEI ALSO PROMOTED GUAN YU TO GENERAL. HE BECAME KNOWN AS THE GENERAL WHO PURGES REBELS.

BUT HE WAS ALSO GIVEN AN ENTIRE *CITY.* LIU BEI APPOINTED GUAN YU *GOVERNOR* OF *XIANGYANG.*

HE THEN ESTABLISHED A *HOME BASE* AT *JIANGLING.*

THAT WAS QUITE AN ACCOMPLISHMENT ... BUT IT PALED IN COMPARISON WITH WHAT LIU BEI HIMSELF DID.

ONCE LIU BEI TOOK JINGZHOU BACK FROM CAO CAO, HE WENT TO *YIZHOU* AND TOOK OVER THE AREA ...

35

... AND A FEW YEARS LATER, HE PROCLAIMED HIMSELF *KING OF HANZHONG*.

LIU BEI FURTHER PROMOTED BOTH GUAN YU AND ZHANG FEI AS WELL.

LIU BEI'S TOP MILITARY LEADERS WERE KNOWN AS THE *FIVE-TIGER GENERALS*, AND GUAN YU WAS FOREMOST AMONG THEM.

IT WAS A GOOD TIME IN THE LIVES OF THE THREE BROTHERS.

BUT IT COULDN'T LAST.

THE PATH TO ENLIGHTENMENT

GUAN YU DECIDED TO TAKE HIS OWN FORCES AND ATTACK THE CITY OF *FAN*, INTENDING TO CONQUER IT.

AT FIRST THE CAMPAIGN WENT WELL ...

... AND IT SEEMED AS IF *NATURE ITSELF* WERE ON GUAN YU'S SIDE.

HEAVY RAINS PUMMELED THE DEFENDERS OF FAN, AND MANY OF THEM DROWNED. ON HIGHER GROUND, GUAN YU MERELY WATCHED.

BUT EVEN AS HE RECOVERED FROM THE POISONED CROSSBOW BOLT, GUAN YU REALIZED VICTORY WAS NOT TO BE HIS.

CAO REN HAD CALLED IN *REINFORCEMENTS*. A HUGE ARMY, FAR LARGER THAN HIS OWN, WAS ON THE WAY. GUAN YU HAD TO RETREAT.

AND EVEN IN THE MIDST OF RETREAT, THE BAD NEWS DIDN'T STOP.

THAT BACKSTABBING, TREACHEROUS *SNAKE!*

WHAT'S WRONG, GENERAL?

OUR HOME BASE IN JIANGLING!

IT'S BEEN *TAKEN OVER* BY SUN QUAN!

IT PROVED TO BE A COSTLY MISTAKE FOR GUAN YU TO LET HIS MEN KNOW ABOUT SUN QUAN'S ACTIONS.

HE EXPECTED THEM TO GO WITH HIM AND HELP HIM DRIVE SUN QUAN OUT AND RETAKE JIANGLING ...

... BUT THE TROOPS GREW *DEMORALIZED*, AND THEY BEGAN TO *DESERT* GUAN YU AND GO OVER TO SUN QUAN'S SIDE.

IN A VERY SHORT TIME, GUAN YU'S ARMY HAD DWINDLED TO A FRACTION OF ITS FORMER STRENGTH.

AND GUAN YU HIMSELF WAS ON THE VERGE OF *DESPAIR*.

WHEN HE SAW SUN QUAN'S SOLDIERS IN FRONT OF HIM, BLOCKING HIS WAY, GUAN YU COULD SENSE THAT HIS TIME HAD COME ...

... AND THOUGH HE TRIED TO GET AWAY, HE QUICKLY SAW THAT HE HAD BEEN CUT OFF.

COME ON, THEN, YOU *SWINE!* YOU FILTHY *COWARDS!* YOU THINK YOU CAN DEFEAT ME?

GUAN YU, THE MIGHTY WARRIOR, REMAINED DEFIANT UNTIL THE VERY END. BUT ON THAT DAY, HIS LIFE AS A MORTAL MAN CAME TO A CLOSE.

IN THAT MOMENT CAME GREAT UNDERSTANDING—

—AND GUAN YU'S SPIRIT ACHIEVED *ENLIGHTENMENT*.

ALL HIS ANGER *VANISHED*, ALLOWING HIM TO FIND PEACE.

SINCE THEN GUAN YU HAS COME TO REPRESENT *HONOR* AND *RIGHTEOUSNESS*, AND MOST OF ALL *BROTHERHOOD*.

AND FOR *THOSE* THINGS WE HONOR HIM. NOW ... AND FOREVER.

GLOSSARY AND PRONUNCIATION GUIDE

AMBUSH: to hide and attack someone by surprise

BLOOD BROTHERS: men who have pledged their loyalty to one another

ENLIGHTENMENT: a peaceful condition in which one feels no suffering or desire

GUAN DAO: a weapon that consists of a curved blade on a long pole

GUAN YU (*gwan yoo*): an ancient Chinese warrior. Guan Yu is an important figure in *The Romance of the Three Kingdoms*, a historical novel that tells exaggerated stories about his life.

LIU BEI (*lee-o bay*): a soldier under whom Guan Yu served. In *The Romance of the Three Kingdoms*, Liu Bei was one of Guan Yu's blood brothers.

MONK: a man who has devoted his life to his religion

MORTAL: a human being, or a being that dies

SIEGE: an attack. To lay siege to a place is to surround it with armed forces.

VENGEANCE (*ven*-juhns): action taken to pay someone back for causing harm

YELLOW SCARVES: a group of peasants that rebelled against the Chinese government in A.D. 184. This group was named for the yellow scarves its members wore.

ZHANG FEI (*jahng fay*): a warrior who served under Liu Bei. In *The Romance of the Three Kingdoms*, Zhang Fei was one of Guan Yu's blood brothers.

original pencil sketch from page 20

FURTHER READING AND WEBSITES

Hume, Lotta Carswell. *Favorite Children's Stories from China and Tibet*. Boston: Tuttle Publishing, 2004. In this illustrated collection, you'll find traditional tales such as *A Chinese Cinderella*, *The Wishing Cup*, and *The Little Hare's Clever Trick*.

Simonds, Nina, Leslie Swartz, and the Children's Museum, Boston. *Moonbeams, Dumplings and Dragon Boats: A Treasury of Chinese Holiday Tales, Activities and Recipes*. San Diego: Harcourt, 2002. Learn about Chinese traditions and holidays through stories, recipes, games, and crafts.

Williams, Suzanne. *Made in China: Ideas and Inventions from Ancient China*. Berkeley, CA: Pacific View Press, 1996. The compass, the abacus, paper, and silk—all these things were invented in China. Learn about these and other Chinese inventions in this fascinating book.

The British Museum: Ancient China
http://www.ancientchina.co.uk/menu.html
This website from the British Museum includes information on five different topics important in ancient Chinese history. It also features several stories and narratives relevant to each of the topics.

China: An Inner Realm
http://library.thinkquest.org/20443/g_home.html
This site is a rich resource for exploring the land, culture, and language of China.

CREATING *GUAN YU: BLOOD BROTHERS TO THE END*

The story of Guan Yu was adapted primarily from *Three Kingdoms: A Historical Novel*, translated by Moss Roberts. Author Dan Jolley wrote the tale in consultation with Wang Ping, PhD, Associate Professor of English at Macalester College, and Wen-Hua Du, MA, of the Department of Foreign Languages and Linguistics at the University of Wisconsin–Milwaukee. Artist Ron Randall relied on numerous historical resources and worked collaboratively with Wang Ping in shaping the story's visual content.

INDEX

ABOUT THE AUTHOR AND THE ARTIST

DAN JOLLEY began his writing career in the early nineties. His limited series *Obergeist* was voted Best Horror Comic of 2001 by *Wizard Magazine*, and his DC Comics project *JSA: The Unholy Three* received an Eisner Award nomination (the comics industry's highest honor) for Best Limited Series of 2003. In recent years, he has cowritten two novels based on licensed properties: *Star Trek SCE: Some Assembly Required*, and *Vengeance*, from the television series *Angel*. May of 2007 saw the debut of Jolley's first solo novel series, an original young adult sci-fi espionage story called *Alex, Unlimited*, published by a joint venture of TokyoPop and HarperCollins. Jolley lives in Cary, North Carolina, where he spends way too much time playing video games.

RON RANDALL has drawn comics for every major comic publisher in the United States, including Marvel, DC, Image, and Dark Horse. His myths and legends work includes *Thor and Loki: In the Land of the Giants*. He has also worked on superhero comics such as *Justice League* and *Spiderman*; science fiction titles such as *Star Wars* and *Star Trek*; fantasy adventure titles such as *DragonLance* and *Warlord*; suspense and horror titles including *SwampThing, Predator,* and *Venom*; and his own creation, *Trekker*. He lives in Portland, Oregon.